DATE DUE

DEMCO 38-297

BASEBALL LEGENDS

Hank Aaron
Grover Cleveland Alexander
Ernie Banks
Johnny Bench
Yogi Berra
Roy Campanella
Roberto Clemente
Ty Cobb
Dizzy Dean
Joe DiMaggio
Bob Feller
Jimmie Foxx
Lou Gehrig
Bob Gibson
Rogers Hornsby
Walter Johnson
Sandy Koufax
Mickey Mantle
Christy Mathewson
Willie Mays
Stan Musial
Satchel Paige
Brooks Robinson
Frank Robinson
Jackie Robinson
Babe Ruth
Tom Seaver
Duke Snider
Warren Spahn
Willie Stargell
Honus Wagner
Ted Williams
Carl Yastrzemski
Cy Young

CHELSEA HOUSE PUBLISHERS

STAN MUSIAL

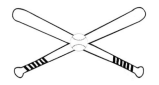

John Grabowski

Introduction by
Jim Murray

Senior Consultant
Earl Weaver

CHELSEA HOUSE PUBLISHERS
New York • Philadelphia

CHELSEA HOUSE PUBLISHERS

Editorial Director: Richard Rennert
Executive Managing Editor: Karyn Gullen Browne
Executive Editor: Sean Dolan
Copy Chief: Robin James
Picture Editor: Adrian G. Allen
Manufacturing Director: Gerald Levine
Systems Manager: Lindsey Ottman
Production Coordinator: Marie Claire Cebrián-Ume

Baseball Legends
Senior Editor: Philip Koslow

Staff for STAN MUSIAL
Assistant Editor: David Carter
Designer: Cambraia Magalhaes
Picture Researcher: Alan Gottlieb
Cover Illustration: Daniel O'Leary
Editorial Assistant: Mary B. Sisson

First Printing

1 3 5 7 9 8 6 4 2

Library of Congress Cataloging-in-Publication Data
Grabowski, John F.
Stan Musial/John F. Grabowski
p. cm.—(Baseball legends)
Summary: A biography of one of baseball's greatest players, Stan "The Man" Musial.
ISBN 0-7910-1184-4
0-7910-1218-2 (pbk.)
1. Musial, Stan, 1920—Juvenile literature. 2. Baseball players—United States—Biography—Juvenile
literature. [1.Musial, Stan, 1920. 2. Baseball players.] I. Title. II. Series.
GV865.M8G73 1992
796.357'09—dc20   91-38207
                                                                                                   CIP
[B]   AC

CONTENTS

WHAT MAKES A STAR

Jim Murray

No one has ever been able to explain to me the mysterious alchemy that makes one man a .350 hitter and another player, more or less identical in physical makeup, hard put to hit .200. You look at an Al Kaline, who played with the Detroit Tigers from 1953 to 1974. He was pale, stringy, almost poetic-looking. He always seemed to be struggling against a bad case of mononucleosis. But with a bat in his hands, he was King Kong. During his career, he hit 399 home runs, rapped out 3,007 hits, and compiled a .297 batting average.

Form isn't the reason. The first time anybody saw Roberto Clemente step into the batter's box for the Pittsburgh Pirates, the best guess was that Clemente would be back in Double A ball in a week. He had one foot in the bucket and held his bat at an awkward angle—he looked as though he couldn't hit an outside pitch. A lot of other ballplayers may have had a better-looking stance. Yet they never led the National League in hitting in four different years, the way Clemente did.

Not every ballplayer is born with the ability to hit a curveball. Nor is exceptional hand-eye coordination the key to heavy hitting. Big-league locker rooms are filled with players who have all the attributes, save one: discipline. Every baseball man can tell you a story about a pitcher who throws a ball faster than anyone has ever seen but who has no control on or *off* the field.

The Hall of Fame is full of people who transformed themselves into great ballplayers by working at the sport, by studying the game, and making sacrifices. They're overachievers—and winners. If you want to find them, just watch the World Series. Or simply read about New York Yankee great Lou Gehrig; Ted Williams, "the Splendid Splinter" of the Boston Red Sox; or the Dodgers' strikeout king Sandy Koufax.

A pitcher *should* be able to win a lot of ballgames with a 98-miles-per-hour fastball. But what about the pitcher who wins 20 games a year with a fastball so slow that you can catch it with your teeth? Bob Feller of the Cleveland Indians got into the Hall of Fame with a blazing fastball that glowed in the dark. National League star Grover Cleveland Alexander got there with a pitch that took considerably longer to reach the plate; but when it did arrive, the pitch was exactly where Alexander wanted it to be— and the last place the batter expected it to be.

There are probably more players with exceptional ability who didn't make it to the major leagues than there are who did. A number of great hitters, bored with fielding practice, had to be dropped from their team because their home-run production didn't make up for their lapses in the field. And then there are players like Brooks Robinson of the Baltimore Orioles, who made himself into a human vacuum cleaner at third base because he knew that working hard to become an expert fielder would win him a job in the big leagues.

A star is not something that flashes through the sky. That's a comet. Or a meteor. A star is something you can steer ships by. It stays in place and gives off a steady glow; it is fixed, permanent. A star works at being a star.

And that's how you tell a star in baseball. He shows up night after night and takes pride in how brightly he shines. He's Willie Mays running so hard his hat keeps falling off; Ty Cobb sliding to stretch a single into a double; Lou Gehrig, after being fooled in his first two at-bats, belting the next pitch off the light tower because he's taken the time to study the pitcher. Stars never take themselves for granted. That's why they're stars.

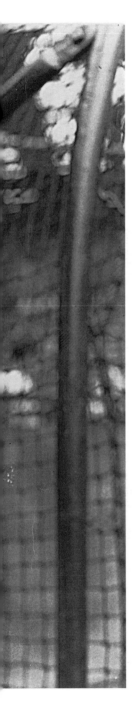

Many baseball fans say that Babe Ruth enjoyed the greatest single season in major league history. In 1921, the legendary slugger finished the year with a set of eye-popping statistics. The New York Yankees outfielder led the American League in home runs (59), runs batted in (171), runs scored (177), total bases (457), bases on balls (144), and slugging percentage (.846). He finished second in the league in doubles (44) and third in batting average (.378). He also collected 16 triples among his 204 base hits.

What Stan Musial accomplished during the 1948 season is nearly as impressive.

That year marked Musial's seventh season in the big leagues with the St. Louis Cardinals. He was 27 years old and, he recalled, "at my athletic peak. . . . The bat felt so light that instead of gripping it about an inch up the handle, as I had in the past, I went down to the knob. Gripping the bat at the end, I could still control my swing."

In the midst of a tight pennant race, Stan Musial poses outside the batting cage on June 30, 1948. Musial was then in the midst of his greatest season, in which he would record career highs in hits, doubles, batting average, slugging percentage, runs scored, and runs batted in.

Musial tore up the National League during the first half of the 1948 season and was batting .410 by the All-Star break. No National Leaguer had ended the season over the .400 mark since second baseman Rogers Hornsby hit .403 for St. Louis in 1925.

Musial continued his hot hitting in the All-Star Game. Sportsman's Park, a stadium shared by the Cardinals and their American League counterparts, the St. Louis Browns, hosted the 1948 contest. The left-hand-hitting Musial started in the outfield for the National League, and he did not disappoint the hometown fans. His first time up, he belted a home run to right-center field—the first round-tripper he ever hit in All-Star competition.

The Cardinals returned to action in third place, six games behind the Boston Braves. Musial's bat cooled off a bit as the season wore on, and by the final month of the season he was hit by a pair of injuries. First he jammed his left wrist going after a fly ball. Then a pitch thrown by Brooklyn Dodgers hurler Carl Erskine hit him on the right hand. Little by little, Musial's batting average continued to drop.

Musial was much more concerned with his team's fortunes than with his personal statistics. So he was especially disappointed that he was not at full strength when, with just a few games left in the season, the second-place Cardinals traveled to Boston to face the front-running Braves.

Standing on the turf of Braves Field before the first game, sportswriter Bob Broeg noted that the flag attached to the right-field foul pole was caught in a strong wind and was flapping in the opposite direction from home plate. When the wind blew the flag that way, any ball hit to right field would carry especially well. Broeg pointed out the flag to his friend Musial and observed that the conditions were ideal for a left-handed hitter who pulled the ball to right field.

Musial held up his injured wrist, which was heavily wrapped in tape. "Yeah," he said, "but I can't hit like this." After giving the matter some thought, however, he decided to throw caution to the winds. He ripped off the tape.

When Musial stepped up to the plate in the first inning, he opted not to swing for the fences. Instead, he swung easily and stroked an outside pitch from left-hander Warren Spahn to the opposite field for a single. Musial's next time up, though, he swung a little harder and smacked the ball for a double.

Musial crosses home plate after crashing a two-run homer in the first inning of the 1948 All-Star Game, which was played in front of his hometown fans in St. Louis. That season, Musial led the National League in seven offensive categories, and he fell just one home run short of winning the coveted Triple Crown.

The slugging outfielder's third trip to the plate pitted him against reliever Red Barrett. The Braves pitcher promptly fell behind in the count, 2 and 0. Aware that he needed to throw a strike with his third offering, Barrett figured that Musial would have the same thought and would be looking for a fastball, the easiest pitch for most pitchers to control. So Barrett tried to trick Musial by throwing a change-up. But Musial, always a smart hitter, outguessed the pitcher: he waited on the ball and blasted the off-speed pitch over the fence.

Musial's hitting clinic was far from over. He collected his fourth hit of the game in the sixth inning, grounding the ball through the infield for a single. On three other occasions in 1948, he had rapped out five base hits in a game. And he was now just one hit shy of equaling Ty Cobb's all-time record of accomplishing the feat four times in a single season.

Musial received just one more chance to bat in the ballgame, and it came against a little-used pitcher, Al Lyons. The Braves hurler started off the late-inning duel by missing the plate on his first two tosses, which caused the players on the Cardinals' bench to hoot and jeer. They wanted Musial to tie Cobb's record, and so they yelled for Lyons to throw their teammate a pitch somewhere near the strike zone.

Lyons's next offering was a little bit outside, but Musial knew he could not afford to be too choosy. He uncoiled his body, lashed out with his bat, and made enough contact with the ball to bounce it through the infield for a record-tying single.

Musial's incredible hit parade was not enough to carry St. Louis past Boston. At the regular season's end, the Braves stood on top of the National League, 6 1/2 games ahead of the Cardinals. Musial, however, had done as much as was humanly possible to stop the Braves, and he was named the winner of the National League's Most Valuable Player Award for a record third time.

In spite of being slowed down by his injuries, Musial finished the 1948 season with a .376 batting average, the highest mark in the majors. (No National Leaguer, in fact, has topped that figure in nearly half a century.) His phenomenal season also saw him lead the league in base hits (230), total bases (429), runs scored (135), runs batted in (131), doubles (46), triples (18), and slugging percentage (.702).

The only key category in which Musial did not lead the league in 1948 was home runs. He hit 39 balls out of the park that year, which left him just one short of the league lead. Actually, he did hit one other home run during the regular season; but rain in the early innings caused the contest to be called off before the game could be declared official. The homer—along with all the other statistics—was erased from the record books. Were it not for the weather, Stan Musial would now be known as the only batsman in modern times to enjoy a season in which he led the National League in every major category.

2

"I WAS ALWAYS PLAYING BALL"

Nowadays, when a sports fan thinks of western Pennsylvania, the first thing that usually comes to mind is the region's tradition of producing outstanding quarterbacks. Joe Namath, Jim Kelly, Dan Marino, and Joe Montana are among the football players who were born and raised in the area. But in the middle of the 20th century, western Pennsylvania was known more for being the home of one of baseball's all-time greats: Stanley Frank Musial.

Donora, one of the region's many small towns, lies in the Monongahela Valley, just 28 miles south of Pittsburgh. It was there, in a small house on Sixth Street, that Stan Musial was born, on November 21, 1920. He was the fifth child—and first son—of Mary and Lukasz Musial.

Stan's father was a Polish immigrant who had come to the United States as a youngster. He went to work in a wire mill in Donora, where he met Mary Lancos, a teenager of Czechoslovakian descent. They were married a short

Stan Musial at the age of 14, when he served as batboy for the Donora Zincs, a local semipro team. By the time he was 15, the slender youngster was pitching for the Zincs and striking out grown men.

Though baseball was always Musial's first love, in his hometown of Donora, Pennsylvania, he starred in several sports. He is seen here, wearing number 16 and standing second from right, in the uniform of the Donora High School varsity basketball team.

time later and started to raise a family on Lukasz's $5.50-a-week salary.

Money was tight around the Musial home, and Stan's four older sisters—Ida, Helen, Victoria, and Rose—helped out wherever they could. So did Stan and his younger brother, Ed, when they were old enough. As a result, Stan learned the value of discipline and hard work at an early age, and these lessons later served him well on the baseball field.

Around the time Stan turned eight years old, he and his family moved into Grandma Lancos's house on Marelda Street. By then, he knew he wanted to be a major league ballplayer when he

grew up. "I can't remember when I didn't play," he recalled years later. "Seems like I was always playing ball."

His next-door neighbor, Joe Barbao, helped the teenage Stan realize his dream. A former minor league ballplayer, Barbao played for and managed the local ballclub, the Donora Zincs. Stan was invited to become the team's batboy.

One day, Barbao asked 15-year-old Stan if he would like to pitch for the Zincs. The player-manager had seen the youngster excel in sand-lot games and knew that he would not embarrass himself. Although Stan stood only 5 feet 4 inches tall and weighed less than 140 pounds, he was stronger than his appearance suggested. He had trained as a gymnast at the Polish Falcons Club, and he had become agile and powerful.

The older Zincs players were skeptical of Stan's ability. But after he took the mound, he made believers of them. In six innings, he struck out 13 batters.

A short time later, Stan hurled a complete game for the Zincs. Still, people had their doubts about his future as a ballplayer. "Musial is too small for steady playing now," read an article in the Donora *Herald.* "He has a world of stuff and a brainy head, but overwork can harm a young player very easily."

The doubts began to disappear when Stan joined the Donora High School baseball team. In his first appearance on the mound during his junior year, he struck out 17 batters in a seven-inning victory over Monessen High School. Following that performance, word about the hard-throwing, hard-hitting youth from Donora began to spread. The St. Louis Cardinals, Cleveland Indians, and New York Yankees began to express interest in the promising southpaw.

Andrew French, business manager for the Cardinals' Class D Monessen farm team, had Stan work out with the club several times under the watchful eye of manager Ollie Vanek. The first scouting report filed by French gave some indication of the youngster's promise: "ARM? . . . Good . . . FIELDING? . . . Good . . . SPEED? . . . Fast . . . Good curveball . . . Green kid . . . PROSPECT NOW? . . . No . . . PROSPECT LATER? . . . Yes . . . AGGRESSIVE? . . . Yes . . . HABITS? . . . Good . . . HEALTH? . . . Good."

Although Stan had his heart set on being a professional ballplayer, his father was not sure it was the right career to pursue. The teenager was an all-around athlete, and several colleges had indicated he might receive an athletic scholarship to play basketball after he graduated from high school. Lukasz Musial wanted to see his son go to college.

French visited the Musial home in late August 1937 and brought a contract with him. Because Stan was not yet of legal age, he needed his father to sign the contract for him. But his father was not impressed with French's proposed $65-a-month offer for Stan to play Class D ball. It took a last-minute plea from the boy's mother to convince Lukasz Musial to let Stan follow his dream.

"All right, Stashu," grumbled his father, using the boy's nickname. "If you want baseball enough to pass up college, then I'll sign." And with that, Stan Musial embarked on a career that would lead him to the Baseball Hall of Fame.

3

"NOBODY CAN BE THAT GOOD!"

Musial (left) with friend and teammate Gene Hillard when the two of them played for the Cardinals' Rochester, New York, franchise. Rochester was Musial's last stop on the way to the big leagues.

In June 1938, Stan Musial received word from the St. Louis Cardinals front office that he should report to the Williamson, West Virginia, team of the Class D Mountain States League. Having never been away from home for any length of time, the 17-year-old went through a difficult summer. It was 240 miles from Donora to Williamson, and the West Virginia town seemed a world away.

Being homesick may have been part of the reason for Musial's rough outing in his first professional game. He showed poor control and lasted only a few innings against Huntington. His next appearance, which came a few days later, was much better. Pitching against Bluefield, he tossed a three-hitter and won the game, 10–3.

Musial was up and down for the rest of the season; he would pitch a good game and then a bad one. His record for the year was 6-6, with a 4.66 earned run average in 20 games. He also pinch-hit a few times and finished 1938 with a .258 batting average.

Despite the teenager's mediocre numbers, the Cardinals were still high on Musial. One report filed on him that year read: "Arm good. Good fastball, good curve. Poise. Good hitter. A real prospect."

Musial returned to Donora after the season to continue his high school education. He finished his senior year just in time to report back to Williamson in the spring of 1939. In fact, he was in such a rush to get back to the team that he did not attend his class graduation. Instead, he had his steady girlfriend, Lillian Labash, accept his diploma for him.

Musial and Labash had met when he was on the school's basketball team; in later years, Lillian would tease him by saying that she first fell in love with his skinny legs. In any event, the couple dated regularly, and by the spring of 1939 they were talking about marriage. They were wed that November, on Musial's 19th birthday.

Early in Musial's second year at Williamson, he experienced arm problems that caused him to get off to a slow start. He bounced back to post a 9-2 mark, which helped his club reach the league playoffs. But his record was deceiving. His earned run average was an unimpressive 4.30, and he continued to experience control problems.

Where Musial really excelled was at the plate. He batted .352 in 71 at-bats.

The following year, the Cardinals promoted Musial to Daytona Beach in the Florida State League. Stan and his new bride promptly moved to Florida, where they were befriended by the team's manager, Dickie Kerr, and his wife, Corinne. "Dickie and his wife treated us like their own children," Musial remembered years later. "He was wonderful. What he did for my morale, I'll never be able to repay."

But Musial did try to repay Kerr for having such a positive influence on his career. When the Musials' first child, a son, was born that August, they named him Richard, after the manager. And years later, after Musial had attained major league stardom, he again showed his gratitude to the Kerrs by buying them a home in Houston.

As delighted as Musial was to have Kerr as his manager, his season in Daytona Beach did not go as planned. One warm August day, he was playing center field when an Orlando player hit a sinking line drive to the outfield. An experienced gymnast, Musial charged the ball and dove, expecting to somersault after making the catch. But his spikes caught in the turf, and he came down heavily on his left shoulder.

The new star of the St. Louis Cardinals signs an autograph for a hometown admirer in Donora, where he worked in the off-season behind the counter of his in-laws' grocery store. In the 1940s, most ballplayers had to take off-season jobs to make ends meet.

Although X rays indicated that no bones were broken, a bad bruise kept Musial out of action for a while. Upon his return, he discovered that his arm was not as strong as it had been before the injury. He hoped that a winter of rest would help it heal.

Kerr, a former major league pitcher, went out of his way to improve Musial's ability on the mound, and the youngster's final statistics showed an 18-5 record for league-leading Daytona Beach. His control problems had continued to plague him, however. And considering his solid .311 average at the plate, it began to look as though he might have a better future as a batter than as a pitcher.

Musial began the 1941 season as the right fielder and cleanup hitter for the Cardinals' Class C Springfield (Missouri) ballclub. That year, he showed some long-ball power at bat for the first time in his professional career. After hitting a total of just 3 home runs in his first three seasons, Musial clouted 26 round-trippers in only 87 games for Springfield. He also drove in 94 runs while hitting .379—numbers that caught the eye of the St. Louis front office.

In late July, Musial was ordered to report to the Rochester Red Wings of the International League in Triple A ball. He was now just one short jump away from the major leagues.

Musial continued his hot hitting for the Red Wings. In 54 games, he batted .326 and helped the club reach the playoffs. Then his grand dream came true: the Cardinals announced that he would report to the big league club after the Red Wings ended their season.

The 1941 Cardinals were in second place, only two games behind the Brooklyn Dodgers, when the 20-year-old Musial joined his new teammates at Sportsman's Park for a double-header against the Boston Braves. Wearing uniform number 6, Musial started the second game and in his first at-bat faced veteran pitcher Jim Tobin, a knuckleballer. Tobin was the first knuckleball pitcher Musial had ever faced, and he popped out weakly to third base.

Musial made some adjustments his next time up and stroked a two-run double. It was the first of his 3,630 major league hits. He got one other hit that day as the Cardinals swept the Braves to stay in contention for the pennant.

Musial clouted his first big league home run against the Pittsburgh Pirates, hitting it in Forbes Field in front of many of his friends and family. Two days later, his fans from Donora staged a Stan Musial Day celebration at the Pittsburgh ballpark. The hometown boy who made it to the major leagues was showered with gifts from his proud neighbors. Unfortunately, the Cardinals were eliminated from the pennant race that same day.

Musial's first taste of the big leagues was a rousing success. The Donora Greyhound, as he was now called, batted .426 in 12 games, collecting 20 hits in only 47 at-bats. Many of the people who saw him play ball that year were echoing the words of Chicago Cubs manager Jimmy Wilson, who had exclaimed: *"Nobody* can be that good!"

4

THAT CHAMPIONSHIP SEASON

In 1942, his first full season in the major leagues, Musial was an important but not a central figure on an extremely powerful St. Louis squad that won 106 games. His .315 batting average was third highest in the National League, but he was not as valuable a contributor to the team's success as shortstop Marty Marion or outfielder Enos Slaughter.

The St. Louis Cardinals began the 1942 season as favorites to win the National League pennant. Despite a rocky spring training, Musial got off to a good start once the regular season began. The Cardinals struggled at times but reached midseason with a solid 47-30 record. Musial was hitting well over .300.

St. Louis may have been playing winning baseball, but the Brooklyn Dodgers were doing even better. The Cardinals trailed their archrivals by eight games. Undismayed, Musial and his teammates were prepared to mount a challenge.

St. Louis was led by a host of veteran players, including center fielder Terry Moore and catcher Walker Cooper, and such younger players as shortstop Marty Marion, third baseman Whitey Kurowski, and right fielder Enos Slaughter. The pitching staff was solid, with Mort Cooper, Howie Krist, Max Lanier, and rookie sensation Johnny Beazley leading the way. By late September, when the Cardinals arrived in Brooklyn for their final series against the Dodgers, the home team's margin over the visitors had been cut to two games. St. Louis won both contests and was tied for first place with only 14 games remaining.

Everything seemed to go the Cardinals' way down the homestretch. Different players, including Musial, took turns being heroes. In one game, his first major league grand slam turned a 3–0 Pittsburgh lead into a 4–3 St. Louis victory. In another game, his ninth-inning base hit drove in the winning run against the Philadelphia Phillies.

By winning the first game of a doubleheader against the Chicago Cubs on the season's last day, the Cardinals clinched first place to cap a miraculous stretch drive. St. Louis had won 43 of its last 52 games to finish with 106 victories. No National League team since the 1909 Pirates had won as many games in a season. Musial finished his first full season in the majors with a .315 batting average, 32 doubles, 10 triples, 10 home runs, and 72 runs batted in.

The Cardinals' World Series opponents were the powerful New York Yankees. The New Yorkers had won the American League pennant by 10 games; most people considered them heavy favorites to win their sixth world championship in seven years.

In Game 1, New York jumped out to a 7–0 lead, only to see St. Louis rally for four runs in the bottom half of the ninth inning. With the bases loaded and two men out, Musial stepped to the plate with a chance to win the game. He wound up hitting a hard ground ball to first base for the final out.

Still, the Cardinals' late comeback proved to be a sign of things to come. They took a 3–0 lead in Game 2, but a three-run homer by Charley

*Musial slides safely into
third base in the fourth
inning of the fourth game
of the 1942 World Series.*

Keller tied the score in the top of the eighth. In
the bottom half of the inning, Slaughter stroked
a double, and Musial drove him in with a single.
The run held up, and the Series was tied at one
game apiece.

The Fall Classic moved to New York's Yankee
Stadium for Game 3, with more than 69,000
fans expecting to see their hometown heroes
regain the lead. What took place was a masterful
pitching duel won by St. Louis left-hander Ernie
White, 2–0. Game 4 saw the bats on both sides
return to life. A total of 22 hits accounted for 15
runs as St. Louis won a 9–6 slugfest. Musial's
contribution was a Series record-tying two hits
in his team's six-run fourth inning.

With their confidence soaring, the Cardinals
took the field for Game 5 and played the Yankees
even, 2–2, through eight innings. In the top of
the ninth inning, Kurowski slugged a two-run
homer. Beazley then set the American League
champs down to end the game, making the
Cardinals world champions for the first time
since 1934.

Musial joined in the madcap celebration in
the clubhouse as the players romped around
and ripped up National League president Ford
Frick's hat. Only 21 years old, Musial could now,
as he put it, "walk down the streets of Donora as
a member of baseball's world champions."

5

THE MAN

Stan Musial's future looked bright as the 1943 season got under way, although the United States was fighting in World War II, and a number of the St. Louis ballplayers had entered into military service. Other ballclubs were in the same situation, and the Cardinals boasted a deeper squad than the rest. They coasted to their second pennant in a row, finishing with an 18-game margin over the Brooklyn Dodgers.

In 1942, as a rookie, Musial had occasionally been platooned by manager Billy Southworth. In 1943, he played day in and day out, and his production was even more impressive. Musial led the National League in batting with a robust .357 mark. His 48 doubles, 20 triples, and 220 hits were also league highs. He scored more than 100 runs for the first of 11 consecutive years. He also hit 13 homers and drove in 81 runs. For leading the Cardinals to the pennant, Musial was voted the National League's most valuable player.

Musial snags a low line drive. Although it was his hitting that won him headlines, Musial was also a fine fielder who played first base as well as the outfield in the course of his career.

The Cardinals' opponent in the 1943 World Series was, once again, the Yankees. This time, however, St. Louis was able to eke out only one win as the Yankees regained the world championship.

Shortly after the Series ended, Musial joined several other major leaguers in a six-week tour of military installations, traveling to Alaska and the Aleutian Islands to entertain the troops. As the father of a young child, he did not have to serve in the military. Still, he was anxious to contribute to the American war effort.

Upon his return to the United States, Musial signed a three-year contract with the Cardinals. In 1944, St. Louis once again won the pennant handily, and Musial contributed a .347 batting average, along with 112 runs scored, 94 runs batted in, 12 home runs, and league-leading totals of 197 hits and 51 doubles.

Life in the big leagues was a matter of great interest to Musial's fellow naval recruits at the Bainbridge Naval Training Center in Maryland in 1945. Most of the great ballplayers of the 1940s lost some time from their careers to military service in World War II.

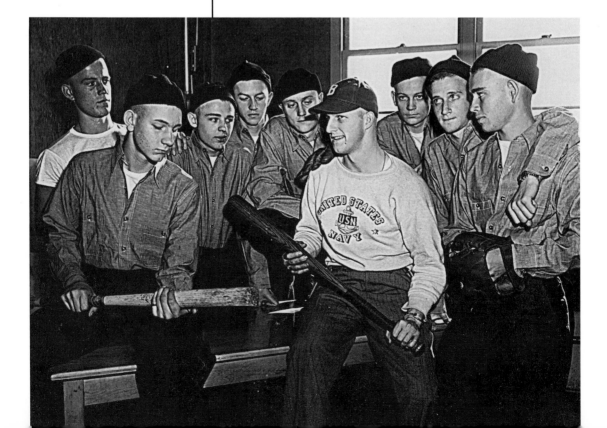

The Cardinals' World Series opponents in 1944 were their crosstown rivals, the St. Louis Browns. For the first time in Musial's brief career, the Cardinals were favorites in postseason play—and they fully lived up to their fans' expectations, winning the Series in six games. Musial batted .304, notching 7 hits in 23 at-bats. His two-run homer in Game 4 was to be his only round-tripper in World Series competition. The $4,626.01 winner's share came in handy for the Musials, whose second child, daughter Geraldine, was born that December.

In January 1945, Musial received notification from his local draft board that he was no longer exempt from military service. He was inducted into the U.S. Navy and reported to Bainbridge, Maryland, for his basic training. During his time in the service, he played baseball for navy teams at both Bainbridge and Pearl Harbor, Hawaii, where he was assigned as a ship repairman.

During his stint in the navy, Musial became aware of the special entertainment value of the home run. Accordingly, he altered his batting stance slightly in order to hit for more power. By the time he was discharged from the navy—just in time for the 1946 season—he was showing promise of being an even better all-around player than before he had entered the service.

Unfortunately for St. Louis, the intervening year had not been as kind to several other Cardinals players. Injuries had taken their toll on Terry Moore, Ernie White, and Johnny Beazley, while Johnny Hopp, Ray Sanders, and Mort and Walker Cooper had moved on to join other clubs. The Cardinals team that took the field on opening day was not the same world championship squad that Musial had left behind.

Despite all the changes, St. Louis was still in contention for the 1946 pennant when the season's most significant event took place. In late May, Mexican businessman Jorge Pasquel and his brothers had been spreading money around in an effort to attract major leaguers to play in a new league in Mexico. The chance to make fabulous sums of money lured Cardinals Fred Martin, Lou Klein, and star pitcher Max Lanier south of the border.

Musial was soon approached by the Pasquels. Despite an offer of $175,000, he turned them down. Manager Eddie Dyer made the clinching argument. "Stan," he said, "you've got two children. Do you want them to hear someone say, 'There are the kids of a guy who broke his contract?'" Musial was rewarded for his loyalty later in the year when St. Louis owner Sam Breadon gave him a $5,000 raise.

Somehow, despite all the distractions, the Cardinals were able to pull together and edge back into the race. In July, they caught the first-place Brooklyn Dodgers by sweeping a four-game series, during which Musial seemed to get a clutch hit every time he came to bat. The next time St. Louis played the Dodgers in Brooklyn, the fans began to chant, "Here comes that man again," whenever Musial came to the plate. The newspapers picked up on it, and Musial had a new nickname: Stan the Man.

The Dodgers and the Cardinals headed down the stretch neck and neck, and when the regular season was over, they had identical records: 96-58. For the first time in major league history, a three-game playoff was held. The Cardinals won

Games 1 and 2, and Musial was on his way to a fourth World Series in his fourth full big league season.

The powerful Boston Red Sox, led by Ted Williams, Rudy York, and Bobby Doerr, represented the American League. The teams split the first six games, leading up to the decisive seventh contest in St. Louis. This game proved to be one of the most exciting in World Series history. The winning run was scored in the bottom of the eighth inning as Enos Slaughter, in a daring feat of baserunning, scored all the way from first on Harry Walker's single to left-center field. A ninth-inning rally by Boston fell short, and the Cardinals were once again world champions.

Although Musial batted just .222 in the Series, he had put together a marvelous year. He

The two premier left-handed batters of their generation—possibly of all time—Ted Williams of the Boston Red Sox (left) and Musial, pose together before the opening game of the 1946 World Series.

won his second batting title, with a .365 average, and also led the league in at-bats, runs, hits, doubles, triples, and slugging percentage. In addition, the now-rising star reached the century mark in runs batted in for the first time in his career. Musial was named the National League's most valuable player for the second time.

After signing a new contract calling for him to receive $31,000 for the 1947 season, Musial looked forward to yet another successful year. His hopes received a setback early in the year, however, when he was diagnosed as having acute appendicitis. After being examined by the Cardinals team physician, Dr. Robert F. Hyland, he received somewhat better news: an operation to remove the appendix could be put off until after the season.

Trapped: Musial puts on the brakes as he realizes he is caught in a rundown between Boston third baseman Pinky Higgins (number 36) and pitcher Dave Ferriss. The play occurred in the first inning of the third game of the 1946 World Series, which Boston won 4–0. The Cardinals bounced back and went on to win one of the most exciting Series ever played.

Musial rejoined the team with high spirits. But by the middle of June, the Cardinals were mired in last place, and Musial was barely hitting above .200. As is often the case with great hitters, he broke out of his slump with a bang, lifting the ballclub in the process. He batted well over .300 for the rest of the year as St. Louis began to make its move in the National League standings.

The team's slow start proved fatal, however. Despite a strong stretch run, the Cardinals could do no better than a second-place finish, five games behind the Dodgers. Musial wound up raising his average to .312. He also drove home 95 runs. But his offensive totals dropped from the previous year in every category except home runs (19).

The season over, Musial had his inflamed appendix and his tonsils removed. As his strength came back, he knew he would rebound with a productive year in 1948. But he had no idea just how great a year it would be.

6

"WALK HIM ON FOUR PITCHES"

After playing mostly at first base during the previous two seasons, Stan Musial returned to the outfield for the 1948 campaign. He started off well and never looked back. "The happiest moment of my life," he said later, "was when I found I could swing with my old freedom in spring training in 1948." His body was free of the troubling low-grade infections that had sapped his strength in 1947.

Musial hit everything in sight in 1948. "I know how to get Musial out," said Brooklyn Dodgers pitcher Preacher Roe. "Walk him on four pitches and pick him off first."

A true team player, Musial always felt that hitting was only part of a ballplayer's job. And he fielded magnificently for the Cardinals in 1948.

Playing center field at Brooklyn's Ebbets Field in September, he somersaulted to make a catch that robbed Jackie Robinson of an extra-base hit. Later in the same game, he sprinted all the way to deep left-center and deprived Pee Wee Reese of another base hit. As a result of these circus catches, Musial's left wrist would remain

The father of Stan the Man: Lukasz Musial poses with his son in the lobby of the New Yorker Hotel. Initially convinced that baseball was an unworthy career, Lukasz came to be extremely proud of his son's achievements.

39

injured for the balance of the season. But he had become such a great professional that not even injuries could stop him.

The year 1948, however, ended on a sad note for Musial. That October, a poisonous smog carried fumes from the zinc works in Donora to the valley where his family lived. Thousands of residents became ill, including Musial's father. Musial brought his parents to live with him in St. Louis, but his father died a short time later.

At about the same time, Musial became friendly with Julius ("Biggie") Garagnani, owner of a St. Louis restaurant. When Musial expressed interest in becoming involved in some sort of business outside of baseball, Garagnani offered him a partnership in the restaurant. Musial accepted, and the partnership developed into a profitable relationship for both men. Musial's name and Garagnani's business sense made the restaurant a successful St. Louis landmark for many years.

The Cardinals were not picked to do much in 1949, and Musial started out slowly. Influenced by his increased power output the year before, Musial began to swing for the fences. "Kiner is right," he said, referring to a quip by National League home run king Ralph Kiner. "Singles hitters drive Fords, home run hitters drive Cadillacs. I'm going for the home run title this year."

The Cardinals stayed in the pennant race, but Musial's batting average suffered because he was trying to hit home runs. He did not return to his old batting style until the season was one-third over. From that point on, he caught fire and finished second in batting, behind Jackie Robinson, with a .338 average.

One of the season's highlights came on July 24, when Musial hit for the cycle (a single, double, triple, and home run in the same game) against the Dodgers. The Cardinals moved into first place that day but slumped near the season's end, losing six of their last nine games to finish second, one game behind Brooklyn. Musial's final marks again included league-leading totals in hits, doubles, and triples, along with runner-up figures in home runs, runs scored, and slugging percentage.

The year, which began with a death of a fam-

Musial and Julius ("Biggie") Garagnani discuss business in the St. Louis restaurant the two men opened together.

ily member, ended with the birth of a new one. The Musials' second daughter, Janet, entered the world that November.

In 1950, Musial got off to his greatest start ever. Playing all three outfield positions in addition to first base, he was hitting .442 going into June. He ended up winning his fourth batting championship, with a .346 average, but the Cardinals finished fifth, 12 1/2 games in back of the Philadelphia Phillies, a youthful team nicknamed the Whiz Kids. It marked the first second-division finish for St. Louis since Musial had joined the team.

The poor showing cost Manager Eddie Dyer his job. Upon his dismissal, he gave Musial a glowing evaluation. "He's the greatest kid I ever met," said Dyer, "unselfish and a team player all the way."

The next year was not much better for the club, which finished in third place behind the New York Giants and the Dodgers. Musial once again led the league in batting. His .355 average justified his status as the highest-paid player in

Musial deals a fastball to the only batter he ever faced as a pitcher in the major leagues, Frankie Baumholtz of the Chicago Cubs.

league history, a distinction Musial achieved with his $80,000 salary.

In 1952, the team again finished third, 8 1/2 games off the pace. Musial connected for his 2,000th career hit that September, becoming the 91st player in history to reach that plateau.

Assured of his third consecutive batting title, and with the Cardinals out of the race, Musial became an unwilling participant in a promotion staged by the club on the season's final day. He was persuaded to be the starting pitcher against the Chicago Cubs, who were mired in sixth place. The one batter he faced was outfielder Frankie Baumholtz, Musial's nearest rival for the batting lead. Baumholtz, a left-handed batter, moved around to the right-hand side of the plate, put the ball in play, and reached base on an error. However, he failed to score.

The onetime minor league hurler ended his major league tour of duty on the mound with a lifetime earned run average of 0.00.

7

PLAYER OF
THE DECADE

In the 1950s, Musial's individual achievements constituted one of the few bright spots for the declining Cardinals. Here, he is presented with a silver bat by National League president Warren Giles after winning his sixth batting championship in 1952.

During the mid-1950s, the St. Louis Cardinals' fortunes continued to decline. The year 1953 began with the ballclub's owner being convicted on charges of income tax evasion, and the team was put up for sale. An offer to buy it was made by a Milwaukee group that wanted to move the team to Wisconsin. Only a last-minute deal with the owner of the Anheuser-Busch brewery kept the team in St. Louis.

The Cardinals stayed in contention until the All-Star break but ended the year tied with the Philadelphia Phillies for third place, 22 games in back of the Brooklyn Dodgers. Despite a slow start, Musial came on with a rush. He finished third in the batting race, even though his average of .337 was a point higher than his 1952 league-leading mark. He collected two safeties on the season's final day to give him exactly 200 hits, marking the sixth—and last—time he would reach that magic number.

In addition, Musial's 53 doubles led the league for the seventh time, while his 105 walks gave him his only league-leading total in that department. He also scored 127 runs, drove in 113, and walloped 30 homers.

The new owners did not scrimp in their efforts to reestablish St. Louis as a contending team. Thousands of dollars were put into renovating Sportsman's Park, renamed Busch Stadium, and additional thousands were spent acquiring new talent. Still, the hoped-for improvement in the standings eluded the Cardinals. Poor pitching was the main reason the 1954 team finished sixth, 25 games behind the New York Giants.

Musial's season, however, was not without its highlights. On May 2, the Cardinals played host to the Giants in an afternoon doubleheader. After walking his first time up in the opener, Musial proceeded to hit home runs in his next three at-bats. In the second game, he walked his first time up, then hit a long fly to center that was caught by Willie Mays. His next two at-bats produced two more homers before he popped out in his final plate appearance. The five home runs in one day was unique in the annals of the game, and it was not duplicated until 18 years later, when St. Louis native Nate Colbert performed the feat.

Musial, in fact, was on a home run binge for the first third of the season. He slugged 20 home runs in the team's first 50 games, putting him slightly ahead of Babe Ruth's record-setting 1927 pace, when the Yankees slugger blasted 60 homers. The Cardinals star finished the year with 35 round-trippers to go with a .330 batting average, 120 runs scored, and 126 runs batted in.

As discouraging as 1954 was for St. Louis, 1955 was even worse. The ballclub started

slowly and by season's end was down to seventh place, more than 30 games off the pace. The showing was the team's poorest since 1909. Although Musial's .319 tied him for second in the batting race behind the Phillies' Richie Ashburn, his numbers went down in every offensive department except stolen bases.

Nevertheless, the regular season saw Musial get his 2,500th career hit. At age 34, the Cardinals star hitter had a shot at becoming only the eighth player in baseball history to reach the 3,000-hit mark.

The All-Star Game also gave Musial a chance to show that he could still rise to the occasion. He led off the bottom half of the 12th inning in a tie game at Milwaukee's County Stadium and slammed Boston Red Sox pitcher Frank Sullivan's first offering into the right-field bleachers. The homer gave the National Leaguers a stirring 6–5 victory.

During the middle of the 1956 season, Musial received a special honor. The *Sporting*

Going, going, gone: Musial connects for his third home run in the first game of a May 2, 1954, double-header with the New York Giants. He would hit two more in the second game, thereby establishing a mark for the most circuit clouts in a single day.

News named him winner of its first Player of the Decade Award. The honor was based on a poll of veteran players, managers, umpires, scouts, owners, writers, and broadcasters.

Later that summer, Musial fell into a slump and experienced what he considered his worst moments as a major leaguer. For the first time in memory, he was roundly booed when he came to bat late in the game. But the fans' true feelings became evident the next day. In an unprecedented action, a group of Cardinals rooters took out a large newspaper ad, apologizing to Musial for the way some fans had treated him.

Musial finished the year with a .310 average, the lowest in his big league career. His power totals were also down, though he did manage to lead the National League in runs batted in with 109. The team's fourth-place finish gave hope for improvement in the future.

In January 1957, at a fund-raising dinner, Cardinals owner Gussie Busch used the occasion to announce that no other Cardinals player would ever wear Musial's uniform number 6. It was the first number the Cardinals had ever retired. And Musial was still an active player!

When the 1957 season began, Musial was optimistic about the team's chances and his own. "I believe I've got a chance to match my life-

A Cardinals team physician shows Musial an X ray of the fractured left shoulder that was to end his consecutive-games streak at 895, in 1957. That season, in which he won his seventh and last batting title, would prove to be Stan the Man's last great year in the major leagues.

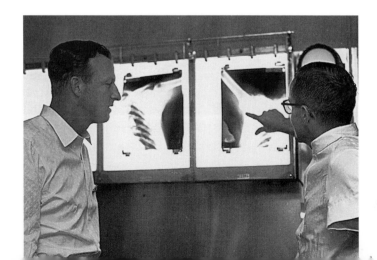

time average," he told reporters with a smile. "That used to mean .350. Now it means .340."

Once again, he had made a minor adjustment in his batting stance, this time to allow himself to hit a slider better. A four-for-four performance on opening day against Cincinnati boded well, and his red-hot hitting continued into June. Meanwhile, St. Louis played .500 ball.

Despite occasional injuries over the years, Musial had missed only 16 games in his first 13 full seasons. His durability came to the forefront later that summer, when he surpassed Gus Suhr's National League record of playing in 822 consecutive games. Musial broke the mark in style, raising his average to .385 with a single and a double in a game against the Philadelphia Phillies.

Musial's consecutive-games streak finally ended at 895, when he fractured a bone and tore some muscles while swinging at a pitch. Unable to throw, he still returned to the lineup for the Cardinals' stretch run for the pennant. Amazingly, he produced 16 hits in 31 at-bats after the injury. But it was not enough to propel St. Louis into first place.

When the pennant was all but decided, Manager Fred Hutchinson told Musial, "You're my Most Valuable Player candidate, Stan. Take off the last three days while I look at some kids. Those other guys couldn't catch you in the batting race if they tried all winter."

St. Louis finished second as Musial won his seventh—and last—batting title with a .351 mark. He drove in 102 runs, reaching the century mark for the 10th time. For his performance, the *Sporting News* named him National League Player of the Year.

8

"BASEBALL'S PERFECT KNIGHT"

The year 1958 began with Musial once again receiving a pleasant surprise. Having completed another excellent year, he told St. Louis Cardinals general manager Bing Devine that he would like to become the highest-paid player in the league. Devine agreed to Musial's request and offered him a contract of $91,000.

Before the formal signing took place, Devine met with the team's owner, Gussie Busch. When Devine got back to Musial, the general manager told the slugger, "I've got pleasant news for you, Stan. Mr. Busch wants you not only to become the highest-salaried player in National League history, but the first to receive $100,000." It was a rare instance of a player being offered more than he had asked for, as well as a show of respect and gratitude to the star.

Musial got off to another hot start, with the added goal of 3,000 hits on the horizon. Although the Cardinals were struggling, he was hitting well over .400 as he approached the magic number.

On May 14, 1958, a throng of fans awaited the return of the Cardinals' train to Union Station in St. Louis, eager to congratulate Musial for recording his 3,000th major league hit, a milestone achieved by only seven big leaguers before him.

After Musial got hit number 2,999 in Chicago, Manager Fred Hutchinson told Musial he would try not to use him the next day—May 13—if at all possible. That way, he would be able to get the big hit in St. Louis in front of the hometown fans. Musial appreciated the move. But when the game was on the line in the sixth inning, Hutchinson was forced to call on Musial to pinch-hit.

Stepping up to the plate in front of fewer than 6,000 fans at Wrigley Field, Musial stroked a run-scoring double off Moe Drabowsky for his 3,000th base hit. With that swing of the bat, he joined Hall of Famers Cap Anson, Ty Cobb, Eddie Collins, Nap Lajoie, Tris Speaker, Honus Wagner, and Paul Waner as the only players in the game's long history to reach the coveted mark.

The hit had special meaning for Musial. "If I had to pick the one big moment of my career," he said later, "that might be it."

Unfortunately, the rest of the season was not as uplifting. St. Louis moved briefly into second place, then fell back as the ballclub's pitchers struggled. They finished tied for fifth, 20 games behind the pennant-winning Milwaukee Braves. Occasionally sitting out the second game of doubleheaders, Musial finished the year with a batting mark of .337 but with his lowest home run total (17) since 1946.

When his daughter Jeanie was born in February 1959, Musial requested—and received—permission to report late for spring training. As a result, he was not in top condition when the 1959 season started. His .270 average at the All-Star break, poor by his standards, led

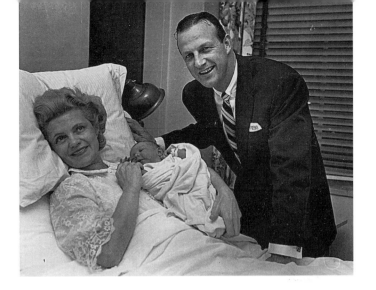

*Musial, baby daughter
Jeanie, and wife, Lillian, in
February 1959. Jean was
the last of the Musials' four
children.*

many to believe that age had finally caught up to
him.

And perhaps it had. Musial started only 92
games and finished with a .255 batting mark.
His totals in all other categories were lower than
usual.

Musial's pride would not allow him to quit
while he still believed he could help the team.
After another slow start in 1960, he bounced
back to hit .275. Although he came to bat only
331 times—his lowest total for a full season—his
marks in nearly every offensive department were
higher than in 1959.

The numbers Musial posted in 1961 were
also respectable. But the Cardinals dropped to
fifth place, and at the season's end, Manager
Johnny Keane spoke to Musial about his plans
for 1962. "Stan," Keane said, "I want you back,
not to play less next year, but to play more."

That his manager thought a 42-year-old
could still be a productive player gave Musial
extra incentive to play for another season. He
worked hard over the winter and reported to
camp in excellent shape. Although the season
was not an outstanding one for the team, Musial

Musial, the greatest National League player of the 1940s, chats with Willie Mays of the San Francisco Giants, the greatest National League player of the 1950s. In the last years of his career, Musial was treated by his peers as an honored elder statesman of the game.

proved he still could do the job. To everyone's surprise, he batted .330 to finish third in the league in hitting. Playing more than in any of the three previous years, he swatted 19 home runs among his 38 extra base hits and drove home 82 runs. He even stole three bases.

Having such a long career, Musial seemed to set a record every time he stepped on the field. He surpassed Honus Wagner's National League record for career base hits, Ty Cobb's major league mark for total bases, and Mel Ott's National League standard for runs batted in. He tied another major league mark when he hit four consecutive home runs over a two-game stretch against the New York Mets, an expansion team, at the Polo Grounds in New York City.

New York fans had always appreciated Musial's talents, and in August he was honored with a special night at the Polo Grounds. That a visiting player should be awarded such an honor indicated the love and respect felt for Stan the Man by fans everywhere.

Soon after the season ended, Branch Rickey, a St. Louis Cardinals senior consultant, was quoted in the newspapers as saying that Musial should retire. General Manager Bing Devine disagreed, thinking that Musial's experience would prove helpful to a young team on the verge of being a pennant contender. Owner Gussie Busch had the final say. "Since when do you ask a .300 hitter to retire?" he demanded.

The ballclub's quick start in 1963 seemed to bear out Busch's words. St. Louis led the league through most of June. But then the club went into a batting slump. By the time of the All-Star Game, Musial knew that age had begun to erode his skills. He spoke to Devine and told him he had decided not to return for the 1964 season. Musial announced his retirement to the public at a team picnic on August 12.

Fans and players alike paid homage to Musial as he made his way around the league for the last time. With the Cardinals 7 1/2 games out of first at the end of August, however, it appeared that Musial's last games would not have much influence on the final standings. But Musial had one more productive month left in him.

The Cardinals won nine games in a row to start September. On the morning of September 11, Musial's daughter-in-law gave birth to a baby boy, Jeffrey Stanton Musial. The next day, on the first pitch he saw as a grandfather, he hit a home run off Glen Hobbie of the Cubs. By the middle of the month, the Cardinals had won 19 of 20 games and had moved into second place, only one game behind the Dodgers, now located in Los Angeles. The Dodgers hung on, however, to win the pennant.

"One of the great heroes of this country" is how President Lyndon B. Johnson (right) characterized Musial on February 14, 1964, in announcing his appointment as national director of the President's Council on Physical Fitness.

On the season's final day, Musial went out on a high note. Baseball commissioner Ford Frick, National League president Warren Giles, and American League president Joe Cronin were all in attendance as Musial was honored prior to his last game in St. Louis.

"This is a day I'll always remember," Musial told the crowd. "This is a day of both great joy and sorrow, the sorrow which always comes when we have to say farewell. My heart is filled with thanks for so many who made these 22 years possible. . . . Baseball has taught me the opportunity that America offers to any young men who want to get to the top in anything. I hate to say good-bye. So until we meet again, I want to thank you very much."

Musial struck out his first time at bat, then grounded a single to right in his second trip to the plate. Coming to bat in the sixth inning of a scoreless game, he hit a single to right, driving home the first run of the game. With the crowd's applause ringing in his ears, he was replaced by a pinch-runner and left the field for the last time as a player. The Cardinals won the game, 3–2— the same score they won by when Musial made his major league debut 22 years earlier.

Although no longer an active player in 1964, Musial remained involved in baseball. He was named a vice-president of the Cardinals and traveled extensively with the ballclub. Later that year, U.S. president Lyndon B. Johnson appointed him national director of the President's Council on Physical Fitness.

The Cardinals finished strong in 1964 and edged the Cincinnati Reds by one game for the pennant. The club then went on to defeat the New York Yankees in the World Series.

The next two years saw the team drop back in the standings, with Musial's longtime roommate Red Schoendienst at the helm. Front-office problems forced Bob Howsam to step down as general manager, and Musial was asked to take over the position in time for the 1967 season.

With pitcher Bob Gibson leading the way, St. Louis ran away with the pennant, then defeated the Boston Red Sox in a hard-fought seven-game World Series. Musial was thus part of a world champion team in his first season as general manager.

That June, Musial was deeply saddened by the death of his business partner, Biggie Garagnani. He asked to be relieved of his duties as general manager so that he could devote more time to his nonbaseball interests.

When Musial became eligible for the Hall of Fame in 1969, no one was surprised that he was elected in his first year of eligibility. That summer, he was inducted, along with Roy Campanella, Stan Coveleski, and Waite Hoyt, on an overcast August day in Cooperstown, New York. Just as Musial stepped up to formally accept the honor, the sun broke through the clouds. "It figured," said Pat Dean, widow of Cardinals Hall of Fame pitcher Dizzy Dean. "The sun always shines on Stan the Man."

In 1966, the Cardinals moved into a brand-new home, Busch Memorial Stadium. A statue of Musial, by Carl Mose, stands in front of the stadium, in full view of everyone who enters the ballpark. The inscription on the statue's base begins with the words: "Here stands baseball's perfect warrior, here stands baseball's perfect knight."

CHRONOLOGY

1920	Born Stanley Frank Musial in Donora, Pennsylvania, on November 21
1937	Signs first professional contract with the St. Louis Cardinals, for $65 a month
1939	Marries Lillian Labash on November 21
1940	Son, Richard Musial, is born in August
1941	Musial makes his big league debut against the Boston Braves on September 17; pops out against Jim Tobin in his first at-bat
1942	Cardinals defeat the New York Yankees in the World Series
1943	Musial named National League's most valuable player; wins first batting title with .357 average
1944	Cardinals defeat St. Louis Browns in World Series; daughter, Geraldine Musial, is born in December
1945	Musial joins the navy
1946	Discharged from military service; receives offer from Jorge Pasquel to jump to Mexican League; named National League's most valuable player; wins second batting title with .365 average
1948	Named National League's most valuable player; wins third batting title with .376 average
1949	Becomes business partner with Julius Garagnani; daughter, Janet Musial, is born in November
1950	Musial wins fourth batting title with .346 average
1951	Wins fifth batting title with .355 average
1952	Wins sixth batting title with .336 average
1954	Hits five home runs in a doubleheader on May 2
1955	Hits 12th-inning home run to win All-Star Game on July 12
1956	Named Player of the Decade by the *Sporting News*
1957	Consecutive-games streak ends at 895; wins seventh batting title with .351 average
1958	Becomes first National Leaguer to sign $100,000 contract; collects 3,000th big league hit on May 13
1959	Daughter, Jeanie Musial, born in February
1963	Musial announces his retirement from baseball on August 12
1969	Inducted into the Baseball Hall of Fame

STANLEY FRANK MUSIAL
"THE MAN"

ST. LOUIS CARDINALS 1941-1963
HOLDS MANY NATIONAL LEAGUE RECORDS,
AMONG THEM: GAMES PLAYED 3026; AT
BAT 10972 TIMES; 3630 HITS; MOST RUNS
SCORED 1949; MOST RUNS BATTED IN 1951;
TOTAL BASES 6134. LED N.L. IN TOTAL
BASES 6 YEARS, SLUGGING PERCENTAGE
6 YEARS. MOST VALUABLE PLAYER 1943-
1946-1948. PLAYED IN 24 ALL-STAR GAMES.
LIFETIME BATTING AVERAGE .331.

MAJOR LEAGUE STATISTICS

St. Louis Cardinals

YEAR	TEAM	G	AB	R	H	2B	3B	HR	RBI	BA	SB
1941	ST. L N	12	47	8	20	4	0	1	7	.426	1
1942		140	467	87	147	32	10	10	72	.315	6
1943		157	617	108	220	48	20	13	81	.357	9
1944		146	568	112	197	51	14	12	94	.347	7
1945					In military service						
1946		156	624	124	228	50	20	16	103	.365	7
1947		149	587	113	183	30	13	19	95	.312	4
1948		155	611	135	230	46	18	39	131	.376	7
1949		157	612	128	207	41	13	36	123	.338	3
1950		146	555	105	192	41	7	28	109	.346	5
1951		152	578	124	205	30	12	32	108	.355	4
1952		154	578	105	194	42	6	21	91	.336	7
1953		157	593	127	200	53	9	30	113	.337	3
1954		153	591	120	195	41	9	35	126	.330	1
1955		154	562	97	179	30	5	33	108	.319	5
1956		156	594	87	184	33	6	27	109	.310	2
1957		134	502	82	176	38	3	29	102	.351	1
1958		135	472	64	159	35	2	17	62	.337	0
1959		115	341	37	87	13	2	14	44	.255	0
1960		116	331	49	91	17	1	17	63	.275	1
1961		123	372	46	107	22	4	15	70	.288	0
1962		135	433	57	143	18	1	19	82	.330	3
1963		124	337	34	86	10	2	12	58	.255	2
Totals		3026	10972	1949	3630	725	177	475	1951	.331	78
World Series (4 years)		23	86	9	22	7	1	1	8	.256	1

FURTHER READING

Burnes, Robert L. "The Magnificent Career of Stan (The Man) Musial." In *Baseball Register*. 1962 ed. St. Louis: The Sporting News, 1962.

Chieger, Bob. *Voices of Baseball—Quotations on the Summer Game*. New York: New American Library, 1984.

Getz, Mike. *Baseball's 3000-Hit Men*. Brooklyn, NY: Gemmeg Press, 1982.

Goodman, Irv. *Stan Musial, the Man*. New York: Nelson, 1961.

Graham, Frank, Jr. *Great Hitters of the Major Leagues*. New York: Random House, 1969.

Gutman, Bill. *Famous Baseball Stars*. New York: Dodd, Mead, 1973.

Hollander, Zander, ed. *Great American Athletes of the 20th Century*. New York: Random House, 1966.

Karst, Gene, and Martin J. Jones, Jr. *Who's Who in Professional Baseball*. New Rochelle, NY: Arlington House, 1973.

Musial, Stan, as told to Bob Broeg. *Stan Musial: The Man's Own Story*. Garden City, NY: Doubleday, 1964.

———. *The Man Stan Musial: Then and Now . . .* St. Louis: Bethany Press, 1977.

Okrent, Daniel, and Harris Lewine, eds. *The Ultimate Baseball Book*. Boston: Houghton Mifflin, 1979.

Shatzkin, Mike, ed. *The Ballplayers*. New York: Morrow, 1990.

Siner, Howard. *Sweet Seasons*. New York: Pharos Books, 1988.

INDEX

PICTURE CREDITS
AP/Wide World Photos: pp. 11, 30, 32, 38; Courtesy Stan Musial: p. 14; National Baseball Library, Cooperstown, NY: pp. 20, 60; *Sporting News*: pp. 16–17, 41, 42; UPI/Bettmann: pp. 2, 8, 23, 26, 29, 35, 36, 44, 47, 48, 50, 53, 54, 56, 58

JOHN GRABOWSKI was educated at the City College of New York, where he was a member of the baseball team, and at Teachers College, Columbia University, where he received his master's in educational psychology. He currently teaches high school math and computer studies on Staten Island. He is a freelance writer who has had several hundred pieces published in newspapers, magazines, and the programs of professional teams. The author of *Super Sports Word Find Puzzles*, *Dodgers Trivia*, *Cleveland Browns Trivia*, *San Francisco 49ers Trivia*, and *Detroit Tigers Trivia*, he published the monthly *Baseball Trivia Newletter*. A nationally syndicated columnist, his weekly "Stat Sheet" is supplied to more than 600 newspapers.

JIM MURRAY, veteran sports columnist of the *Los Angeles Times*, is one of America's most acclaimed writers. He has been named "America's Best Sportswriter" by the National Association of Sportscasters and Sportswriters 14 times, was awarded the Red Smith Award, and was twice winner of the National Headliner Award. In addition, he was awarded the J. G. Taylor Spink Award in 1987 for "meritorious contributions to baseball writing." With this award came his 1988 induction into the National Baseball Hall of Fame in Cooperstown, New York. In 1990, Jim Murray was awarded the Pulitzer Prize for Commentary.

EARL WEAVER is the winningest manager in Baltimore Orioles history by a wide margin. He compiled 1,480 victories in his 17 years at the helm. After managing eight different minor league teams, he was given the chance to lead the Orioles in 1968. Under his leadership the Orioles finished lower than second place in the American League East only four times in 17 years. One of only 12 managers in big league history to have managed in four or more World Series, Earl was named Manager of the Year in 1979. The popular Weaver had his number 5 retired in 1982, joining Brooks Robinson, Frank Robinson, and Jim Palmer, whose numbers were retired previously. Earl Weaver continues his association with the professional baseball scene by writing, broadcasting, and coaching.